LEARN TO DRAW

DISNEY · PIXAR

WALL·E

Illustrated by The Disney Storybook Artists

Inspired by the character designs created by Pixar Animation Studios

Walter Foster

DISNEY · PIXAR
WALL·E

Imagine life in the twenty-ninth century on Earth— this is when our story begins. There are no humans on the planet in the year 2805. Earth is so polluted by trash that all the people left centuries earlier to live in outer space. But this story is less about people than it is about one single trash-compacting robot: a Waste Allocation Load Lifter—Earth class, or WALL•E.

Tiny WALL•E was programmed to do one thing: collect and compact trash until humans could return to Earth and live there once again. But WALL•E wanted to do more than clean up Earth—he wanted to find true love. And thanks to his great big robotic heart, he managed to change—and save—the entire universe.

For centuries, WALL•E lived alone on Earth with his pet cockroach. He gathered trash into his small chest cavity and compacted it into small cubes. Then he stacked the cubes into high towers—a slow but effective process of cleaning up Earth.

WALL•E had other interests too. One of his favorite things to do was to watch videos of old romantic movies; another was to search for interesting items to collect from the trash. This was unusual for a robot. WALL•E thought—and felt—outside of the job he was programmed to perform.

One day EVE—an Extraterrestrial Vegetation Evaluator—arrived. She was a sleek, modern, state-of-the-art robot. Twice WALL•E's size, EVE was egg shaped with a glossy white exterior and blue eyes. WALL•E fell in love at once.

But when EVE saw a little plant that WALL•E had found in the trash, she yanked it away from him and then instantly shut down. WALL•E could not wake her.

Soon after, a ship returned and took the sleeping EVE away. Without a second thought, WALL•E grabbed onto

3

the outside of the ship and went with her. He would follow her anywhere—and he did; right onto a huge luxury space liner called the *Axiom*.

The human passengers aboard the *Axiom* had devolved over the years, growing lazy because robots and other electronic devices met all of their needs and desires. WALL•E changed that. As he chased EVE throughout the giant ship, he accidentally set off a string of events that caused all of the passengers—enough to fill a small city—to open their eyes and become interested in life again.

It started when EVE was taken to the Captain's bridge. The Captain pushed a button, and she awoke—and delivered the plant! WALL•E was happy because he loved her. The Captain was happy because the plant

was proof that Earth could once again sustain life.

But the controller of the ship, Autopilot, had a different directive— he had been programmed to ensure that the *Axiom* never returned to Earth. EVE was determined to fight against Autopilot's directive—and WALL•E wanted to help her.

Eventually, everyone else on the ship joined the fight. The Captain was the first human to leave his hover chair and . . . WALK! Many others followed.

Robots overrode their directives and released the humans from their electronic surround systems. Free to think on their own, everyone saw that they needed to help WALL•E and EVE.

In the end, WALL•E sacrificed his little robotic body to help EVE complete her directive. But EVE's joy in allowing the *Axiom* to return to Earth was overcome by loss—she had fallen in love with WALL•E.

Luckily, robots can be repaired—and they can repair one another. Once back on Earth, EVE worked hard to save WALL•E. And soon he was his old self again—happy, innocent, and in love.

Eventually people returned to live on Earth. There was still a lot of work to do, but WALL•E had shown everyone that with a little gumption and a lot of heart, even a trash-bot can change the universe, making it a better place to live . . . and thrive.

TOOLS AND MATERIALS

Before you begin your drawing, you will need to gather a few simple tools. Start with a regular pencil so you easily can erase any mistakes. Make sure to have an eraser and a pencil sharpener too! When you are finished drawing, use colored pencils, markers, or crayons to bring your characters to life!

drawing pencil and paper

sharpener

eraser

colored pencils

felt-tip markers

paintbrush and paints

HOW TO USE THIS BOOK

By following these simple steps, you'll be drawing WALL•E and his friends in no time!

First draw the basic shapes in the middle of the paper so you don't run out of room.

Each new step is shown in blue, so just draw all the blue lines that you see.

Continue to follow the blue lines to add the details.

Darken the lines you want to keep and erase the rest.

Step 5
Add vivid colors to bring your drawing to life on paper!

WALL•E

WALL•E is a Waste Allocation Load Lifter—Earth class. Although considered a bit ancient for the twenty-ninth century, WALL•E is programmed with a strong directive: to collect and compact trash to clean up the overly polluted Earth. His boxy middle contains his compacting unit; his mechanical arms were designed to gather trash; and his triangular-shaped treads cover the wheels that help him maneuver over the rugged, trash-covered terrain.

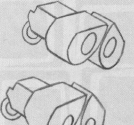

YES!
eyes stay in middle
of face

NO!
they don't move
around on head

Step 1

Step 2

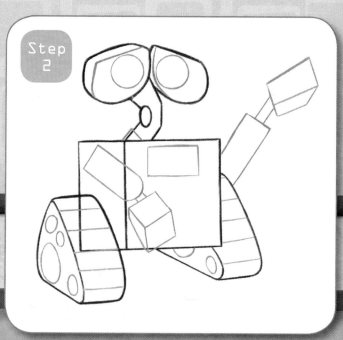

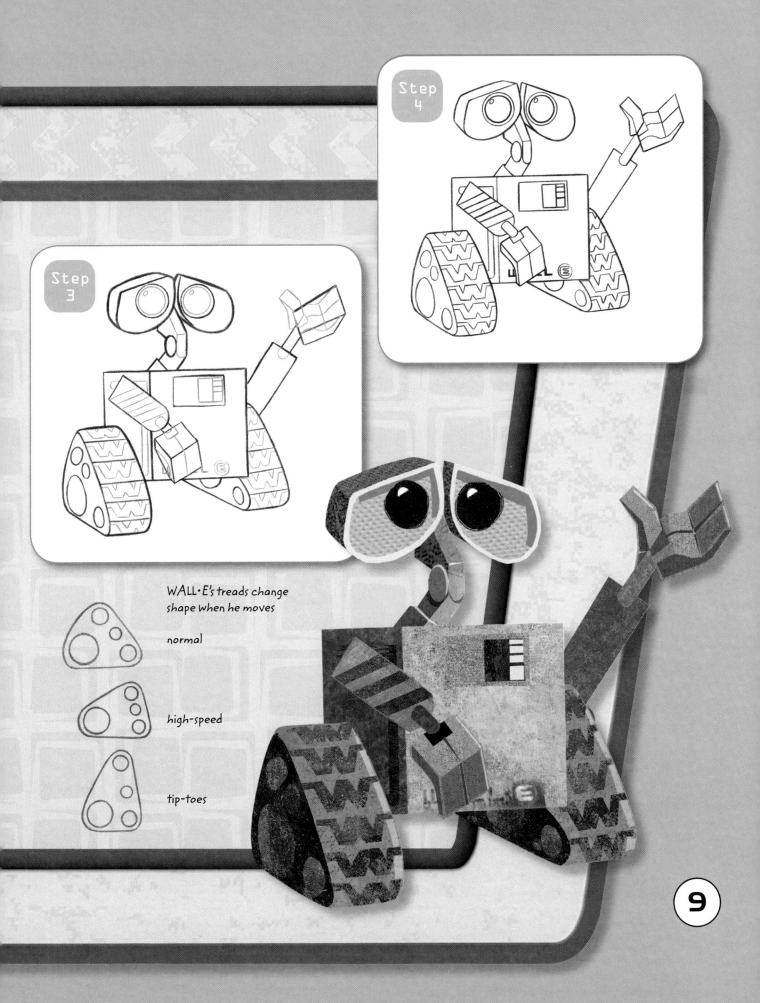

Step 3

Step 4

WALL·E's treads change
shape when he moves

normal

high-speed

tip-toes

9

EVE

EVE is a probe-bot—an Extraterrestrial Vegetation Evaluator. That means she was programmed with the directive to find vegetation on Earth. If she finds a single plant on Earth, humans can return from their space travels and live on Earth again. A growing plant means the Earth's polluted environment can once again sustain life!

facial expressions

neutral

worried or sad

skeptical

laughing

Step 1

Step 2

chest compartment can open

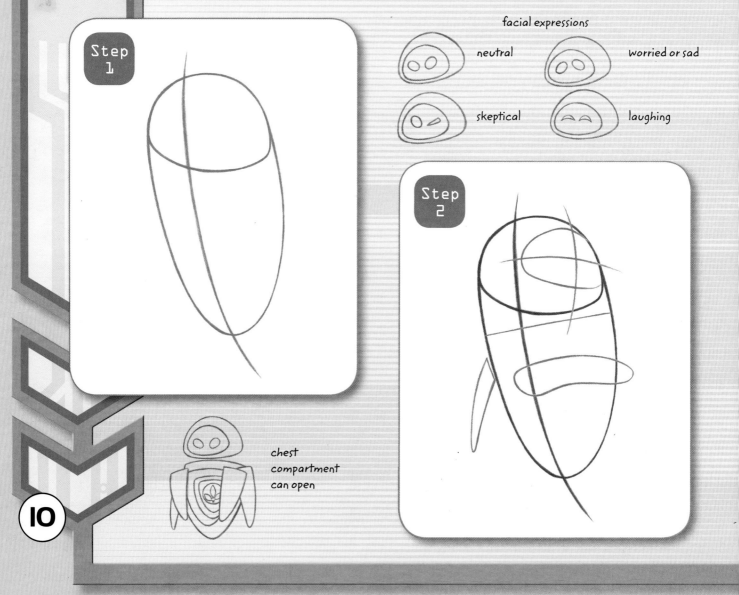

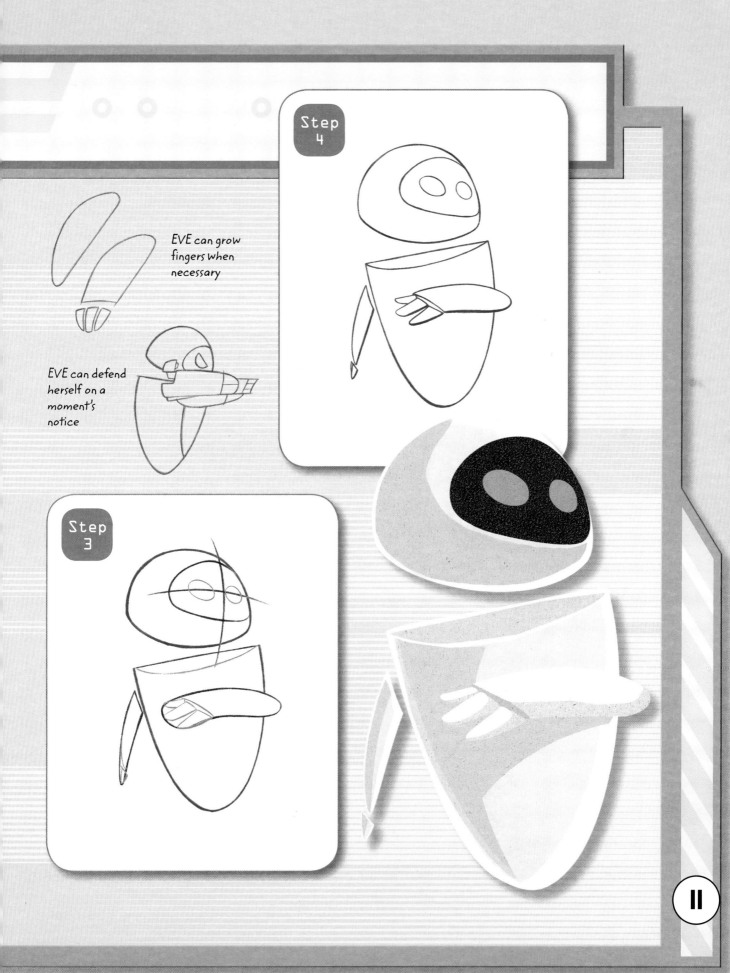

Step 4

Step 3

EVE can grow fingers when necessary

EVE can defend herself on a moment's notice

11

WALL•E AND EVE

WALL•E and EVE may look like an unlikely couple, but it seems that they were meant to be together. EVE is glamorous (well, at least by robot standards), state-of-the-art, and sleek. WALL•E is small, boxy, and dirty. But when they are together, their love is strong enough to overcome their robotic programming. They can send electronic arcs of energy between their heads—robot kisses!

Step 1

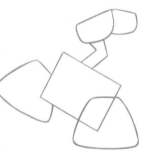

WALL•E's eyebrows can point up or straight across, but never down

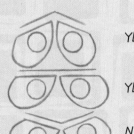

YES!

YES!

NO!

Step 2

WALL·E can squish down into himself when he's afraid

Step 4

Step 3

13

THE CAPTAIN

The Captain, like all the human passengers on the *Axiom*, is a victim of the devolution of humanity caused by a combination of nonstop consuming over the centuries and the distractions aboard the luxury space liner. Barely having to lift a finger to do anything (except to press a button for service), the Captain can hardly walk. And that is why his large, round body and chubby limbs look the way they do. But don't let his appearance fool you. After being accidentally pushed by WALL•E, the Captain proves to be a man of determination—the first in years to actually rise from his hover chair and walk in order to save his ship and passengers.

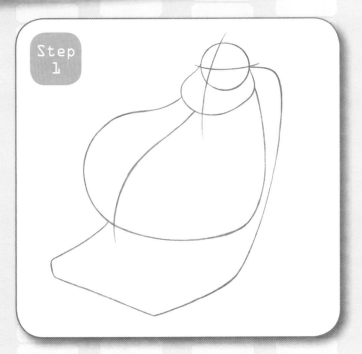

Step 1

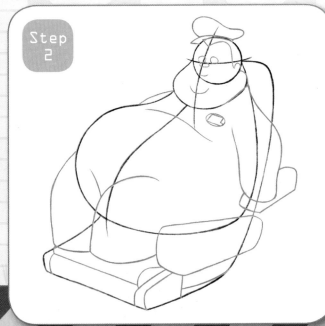

Step 2

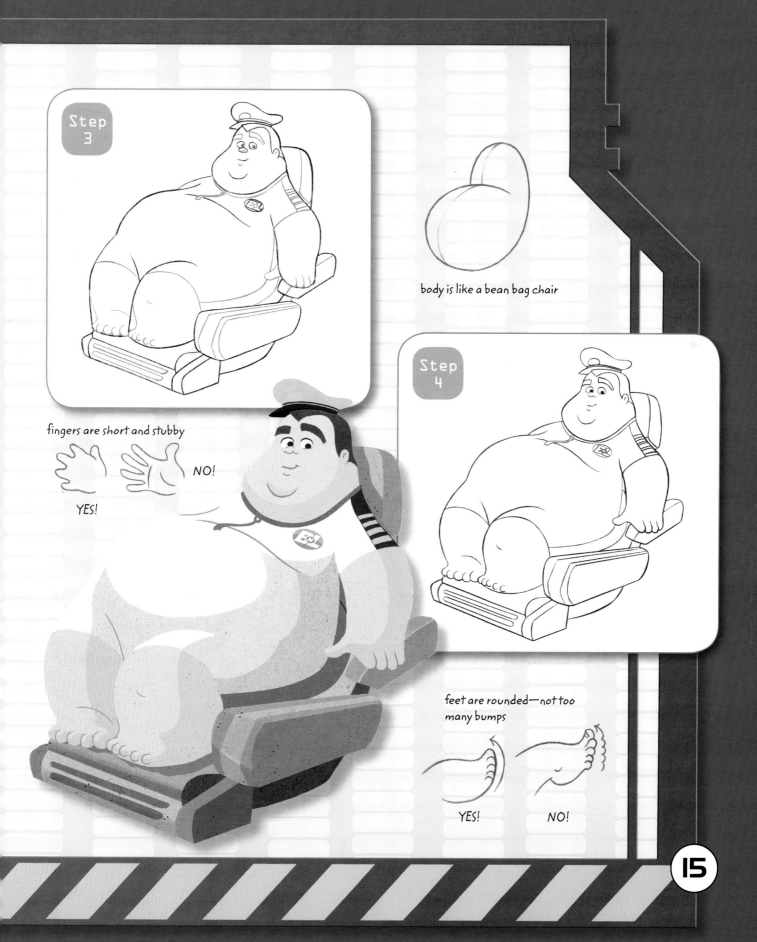

Step 3

body is like a bean bag chair

fingers are short and stubby

YES!　　NO!

Step 4

feet are rounded—not too many bumps

YES!　　NO!

15

AUTOPILOT

The ship's autopilot, nicknamed Auto, has complete control over the ship. Shaped like a ship's wheel with a large eye in its center, Auto is attached to a long, electronic neck device that allows him to maneuver around the ship's bridge. He steers the ship and looks out the windows into space with his big eye, but he's not as innocent as he seems. When his real (and very evil) directive is discovered, he uses his robotic "finger" device not only to push buttons but also to poke the Captain in the eye!

Autopilot resembles an old ship's wheel

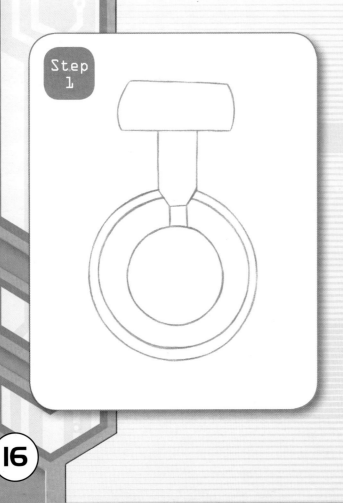

Step 1

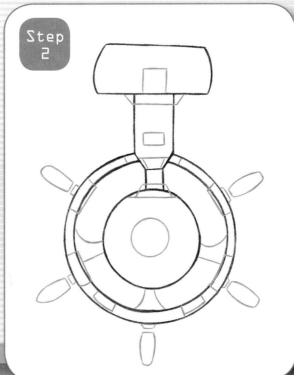

Step 2

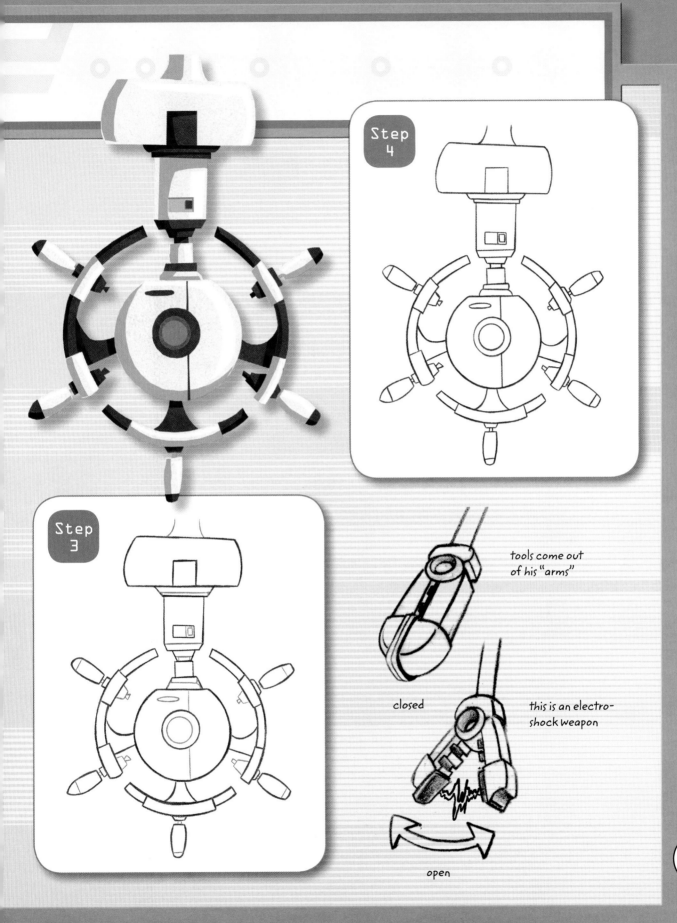

Step 4

Step 3

tools come out of his "arms"

closed

this is an electro-shock weapon

open

GO-4

light inside head flashes in an emergency

GO-4 is a robot that is supposed to serve the Captain and Auto, all for the good of the ship and its passengers. But once Auto is given his evil directive (never to steer the *Axiom* back to Earth), GO-4 becomes Auto's minion. With a siren on his head, GO-4 doesn't hesitate to declare an emergency to try to stop WALL•E and EVE—or anyone else who might try to help send the *Axiom* back to Earth.

Step 1

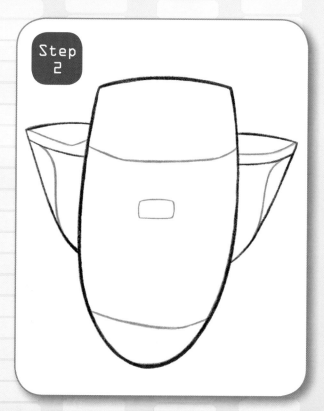

Step 2

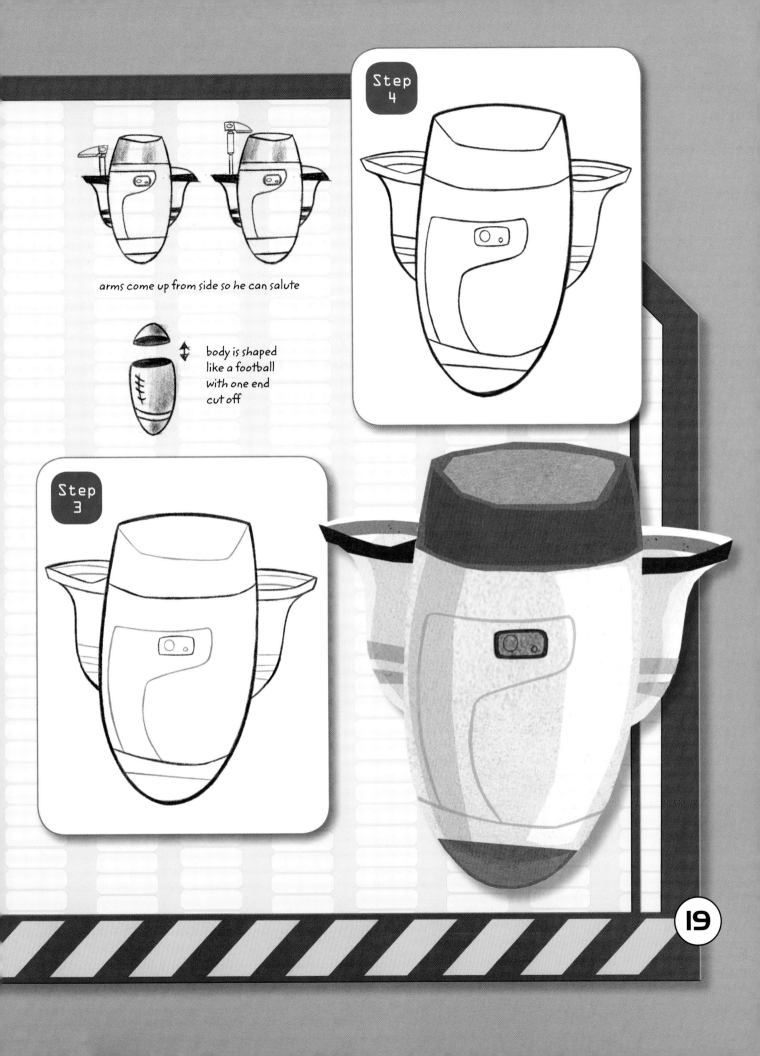

arms come up from side so he can salute

body is shaped like a football with one end cut off

M-O

M-O is a Microbe Obliterator, or a cleaner-bot. In fact, he is so obsessed with cleaning that he cannot stop himself from tracking down the very dirty WALL•E with a vengeance. Ultimately, though, the little guy cannot help liking WALL•E. They even become friends— but only as long as M-O can use his scrubbing brushes to keep WALL•E clean and shiny.

M-O is about half the size of WALL•E

Step 1

Step 2

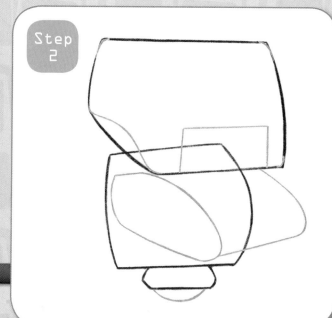

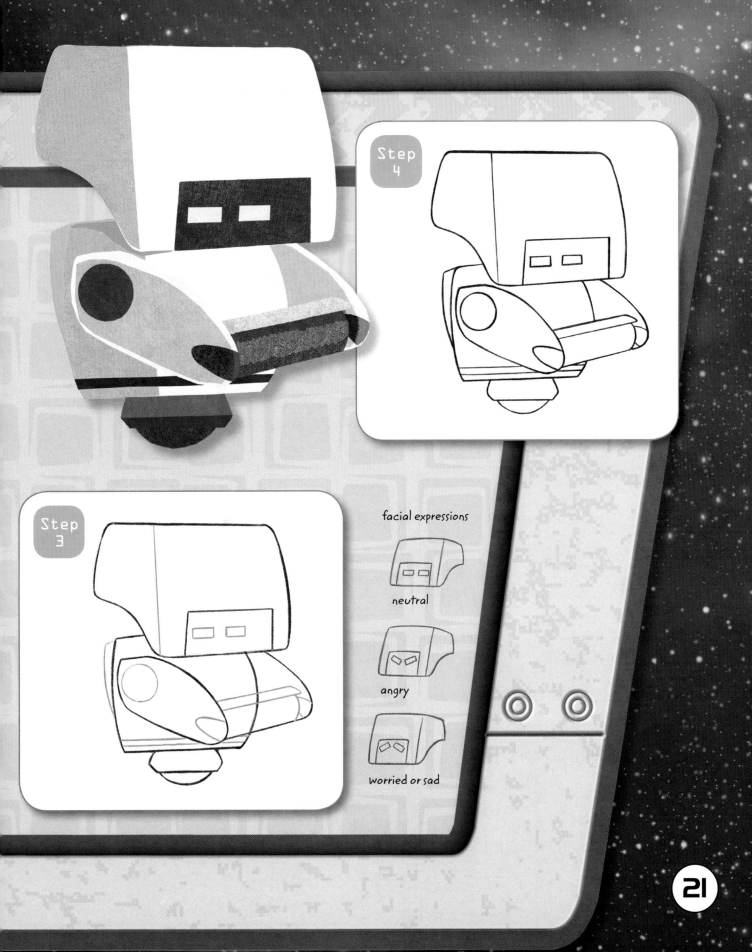

Step
4

Step
3

facial expressions

neutral

angry

worried or sad

BEAUTICIAN-BOT AND VACUUM-BOT

Some robots go to the repair ward on the *Axiom* for quick tune-ups and then go back to work. Others stay there for a long time. Not knowing that they are malfunctioning and in need of major overhauls, these reject-bots are held captive in the repair room. The beautician-bot puts horrible makeup on the faces of humans and robots alike, and the vacuum-bot may clean the dirt, but he sneezes it right back out again.

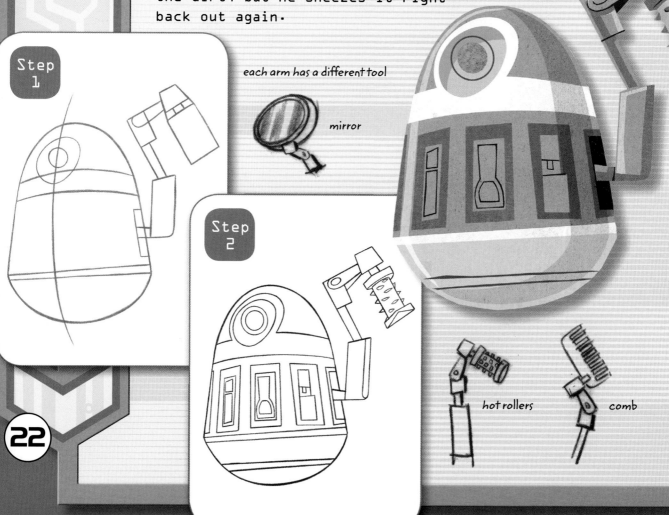

Step 1

Step 2

each arm has a different tool

mirror

hot rollers

comb

Step 1

neck is like an accordion

head consists of a small shape on top of a bigger shape

Step 2

canister in his back shows what he has vacuumed up

23

STEWARD-BOTS AND PAINT-BOTS

The *Axiom's* many steward-bots can broadcast news aboard the ship, capture information with their cameras, and round up rogue robots when necessary, among their other services. The steward-bots are kind of like security guards. Their force is much larger than the paint-bots, who are called on to perform routine painting duties but sometimes end up painting things they shouldn't!

Step 1

Step 2

paint on brush
is thick and
gloppy

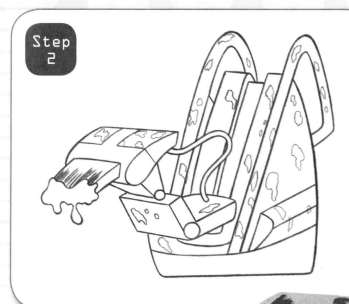

brush can switch to a roller
if necessary

UMBRELLA-BOTS AND LIGHT-BOTS

There are a lot of robots on the *Axiom*, and they are all programmed to do certain jobs. In fact, there is practically nothing that humans ever need to do by themselves! The umbrella-bot is designed to open and close at any human's command. The light-bots turn on and off as needed.

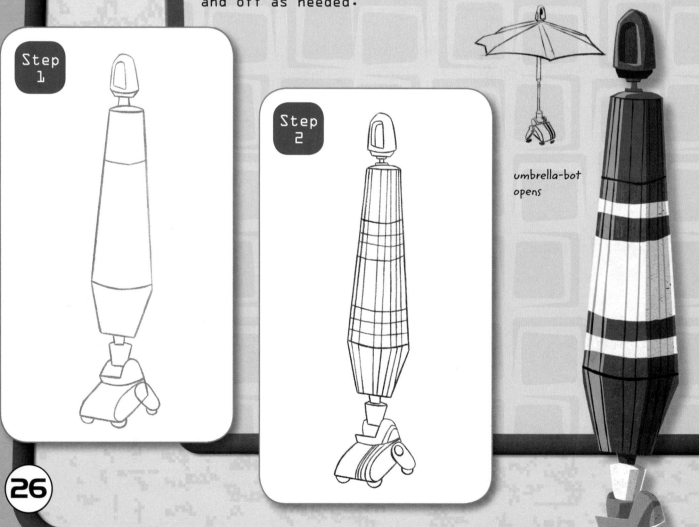

Step 1

Step 2

umbrella-bot
opens

Step 1

Step 2

neck is flexible

27

JOHN AND MARY

This happy human couple may never have met if it hadn't been for WALL•E. Boxed into their hover chairs and surrounded by speakers and video screens, John and Mary are unaware even of the people right next to them. But when WALL•E accidentally disables Mary's electronics, she sees her surroundings for the first time. The more fascinated she becomes with the world around her, the more she wants to share it with someone else. When she sees WALL•E and EVE space-dancing out the window, she grabs the first person she sees—John—and disables his electronics. He too is fascinated by the world around him. And when he turns his head for the first time to see who is sitting next to him, he sees Mary.

ears are
small

YES!   NO!

Step 1

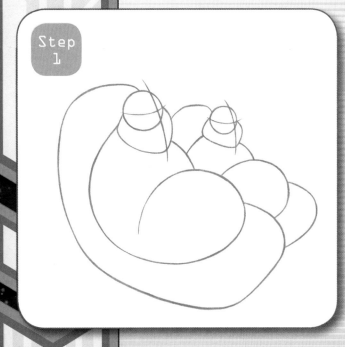

Step 2

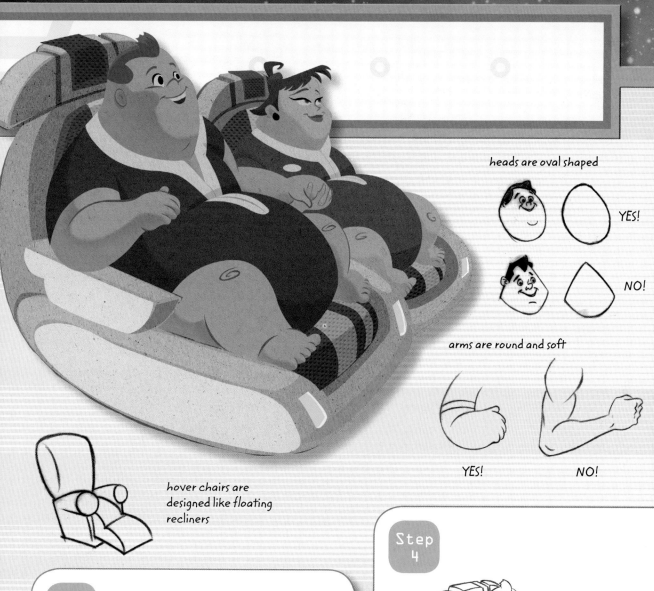

heads are oval shaped

YES!

NO!

arms are round and soft

YES!   NO!

hover chairs are designed like floating recliners

Step 3

Step 4

WALL·E's STORAGE TRUCK

At the end of each day, WALL·E returns to the abandoned truck he moved into years ago and safely shuts himself inside. WALL·E's "home" is filled with interesting trash treasures he finds during his work day, including his favorite video.

tires are flattened out, not round

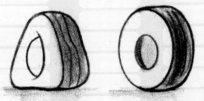

YES!   NO!

angles on windows are sharp

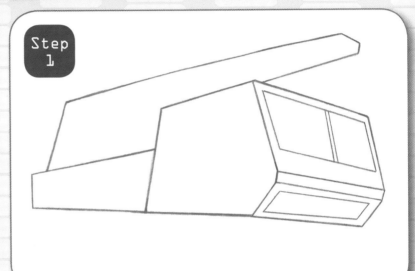

Step 1

Step 2

30

Step 3

pieces of junk from WALL·E's world

paddle ball

trash cube

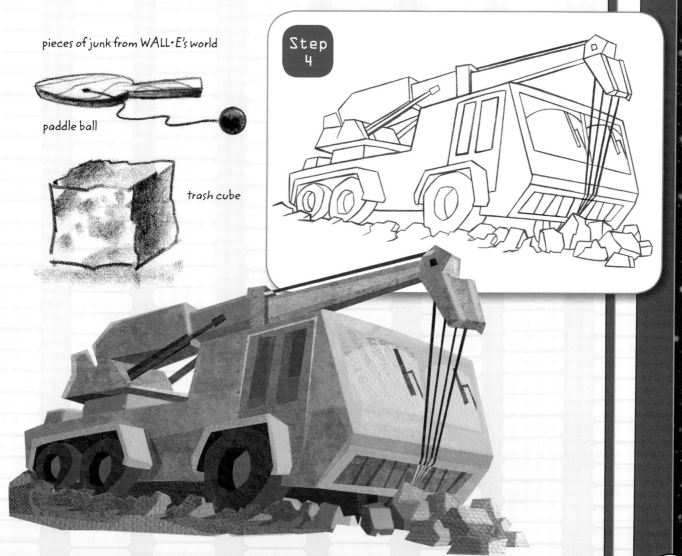

Step 4

WALL·E's WORLD

As you continue drawing, think about WALL•E's expressive face. And don't forget about his heart—that little electronic device that somehow propelled him to follow a dream instead of a directive, thereby returning the heart and soul to Earth and its people.